MIND BODY SPIRIT

MIND BODY SPIRIT

The Ultimate Motivation Guide for the 21st Century

Barry Gohil BSc (HONS)

authorHOUSE®

AuthorHouse™
1663 Liberty Drive
Bloomington, IN 47403
www.authorhouse.com
Phone: 1-800-839-8640

Published by AuthorHouse   10/24/2012

ISBN: 978-1-4772-3915-5 (sc)
ISBN: 978-1-4772-3916-2 (e)

CONTENTS

PREFACE

Barry Gohil has featured in Docklands Newspaper, Men's Health, won the Men's Health Fat Burners Award and featured on BBC Essex Radio, a radio station in the USA and was invited to Department of Health in the UK.

He is the creator of a website called www.breakfastbarry.com.

Barry Gohil is a qualified YMCA qualified personal trainer.

Since the credit crunch he has met over 2000 people who motivated him to write this book.

His first book was called the Breakfast Barry Story published in 2010 and he held a book singing a Waterstones in Ilford, Essex.

The Credit Crunch Story, his 2nd book is based on factual and true events since September 2008.

It is where health and fitness meets creativity and spirituality.

The book will appeal to people impacted by the credit crunch.

WHO ARE YOU? IS THIS YOU?

1. Are you a business person?

2. Have you been affected by the credit crunch?

3. Have you lost a relationship?

4. Have you been made redundant?

5. Have you lost a partner or child?

6. Have emotions got the better of you?

7. Are you unemployed?

8. Financially stressed?

9. Banks screwed up your life?

10. Are you in debt?

11.   Are you a property investor?

12.   Are you a fitness coach?

13.   Has more than one life event affected you?

ACKNOWLEDGEMENTS

I would like to thank Coleridge Williams, Ester Solomons and Nein Sharif and Steffi Nestavalova, Tarinder Singh and God for providing me with life's challenges.

INTRODUCTION

Barry Gohil brings you Mind, Body, Spirit.

It is dedicated to the many people who he came into contact with in person and to all the people who he read about when the Credit Crunch set in September 2008.

Before the Credit Crunch in September 2008 the people he med had picture perfect lives, goals and dreams and high expectations.

During the Credit Crunch Barry Gohil met people who made it all or lost it all from all walks of life. They experienced:

- **BREAKDOWN OF RELATIONSHIPS,**
- **GOT MADE REDUNADANT,**
- **FILED FOR BANKRUPTCY,**
- **SUFFERED LOSS OF INCOME.**
- **EXPERIENCED MORE THAN ONE STRESSFULL EVENT**

People turned to poisons: Junk foods, drugs, drinks, some were even driven to the brink suicide.

Off the may people he met only a few were leading a life of their dreams.

THE CREDIT
CRUNCH

TIME FRAME: SEPTEMBER 2008 TO FEBRUARY 2009

This real life story is based on a man called Brad and his partner Angelina, and his parents: Don and Maria and Brad's son: Kai.

The Credit Crunch set in life tsunami, Brad's redundancy was announced after having worked for a major American bank in London for 11 years.

Brad left London to live a dream life with his pregnant partner Angelina and his parents Don and Maria who had been running a shop that Brad took a risk in buying in September 2007.

So Brad rented his place in London and made a move up north: Midlands. The shop which he purchased was refurbished using his redundancy monies.

Brad was confident that his plan to raise half a million would succeed so that he could use the monies for debt consolidation, to live on a farm in another location and watch his baby grow up as well as work in the shop.

But the dream began to collapse when the banks collapsed. It was the day that the banks ran out of money. The day banks were bailed out by 50 billion.

Banks lending criteria changed. Banks were not lending.

Brad had over 20 people renovating the shop at the same time his baby boy called Kai was born.

Brad was expected to be at the shop as well as be there for the baby and his partner who lived at different location.

Every time there was an appointment for the baby his father—Don also would have a medical appointment. Brad found himself in a catch 20-22 situation. How could he please his partner Angelina and his parents. Conflicts started to arise.

Every time Brad would be at the shop there would be arguments and every time he would be with Angelina he would face the music there too. Compounded with his was the Credit Crunch where Brad found he had borrowed more, and due to change in the banks' lending criteria he could no longer afford to meet his financial commitments.

Unknown to him he was also losing income in London where his so called friends rented out his property and were pocketing large sums of rent.

Brad found himself in a state where he was being pulled in several directions by Angelina, Don and Maria. Also, the Credit Crunch was adding financial pressure.

It was domino effect, a downward spiral, collapse of the banks, he was unable to manage Angelina's, Don's and Maria's expectations. He was asked the help of his brother and he also created new challenges for him.

Brad went to an entrepreneurs convention where there were 200 businesses: banks, businesses from every sector, Brad had meetings with over 20 banks however they could not help in any way.

Fear of loss and bankruptcy was setting in. Brad started to drink heavily, on one occasion following a family conflict he drove at speeds of over 100 miles per hour and found himself sleeing near rail tracks.

He also started experiencing mechanical failures, his car would stop, and his PDA kept of crashing.

He started to experience tension headaches. His health started failing. If was as if someone had cursed him.

It was a time of decepticons—people who did not seem as they were: the banks, friends, by standards, family, and friends—where words had a damaging impact. The word 'Trust Me' had a double edged meaning.

It was also a period characterised by mechanical failures of mobile phone, car and minor accidents.

It was time where more than six things went wrong for Brad in a space of a few months.

Lesson 1:

"When all the odds are against you, when there is no way out. What do you do?"

THE EVIL EYE

Time: September 2008 - February 2009

IT WAS TIME OF THE EVIL EYE

Amidst the credit crunch Brad became a father. Present at the birth was Angelina and her sister Cruela.

With the birth of Kai, female jealousy set in on the part of Cruela; Brad was stuck in the Shop, whilst Angelina was at home with Kai.

Brad expected Cruela to support Angelina and the baby—however this did not happen. Despite the fact that Angelina sacrificed a few years of her life look after a depressed suicidal Cruela.

Angelina was becoming resentful for the key people in her life Brad and Cruela were not there for her and Kai.

Angelina renovated the farm with the help of a builder called David who happened to be Brad's friend.

The idea was for Brad, Angelina and Kai to live happily ever after on the farm.

However Brad knew he could not afford the mortgage of 2000 per month. Especially with financial loss in London and with the shop having loans against it.

Brad found himself to be a nervous wreck and he started to drink. He let his guard down and told David his problems.

Unknown to Brad, David played on Brad's weakness and played the love card in front of Brad for Angelina.

Angelina fell for David's love card. Brad had an intuitive feeling by the way David and Angelina were looking at each other but he could not put a finger on matters as he was not in a state of mind where he could think straight.

David was aware of Brad and Angelina's wealth, David was an illegal immigrant and so took advantage of the situation.

Brad was the subject of the evil eye.

Close friends wanted to be even closer and wanted to take from within.

It was time of spiritual demons, evil prayers and thoughts.

People looking in perceive that you have it all but they do not realize the years of hard work, energy that goes into building and creating.

It was period of confusion, being pulled, hurtful words.

Lesson 2:

"The evil eye exists be aware of it."

IT WAS TIME OF FIGHTING LOVE

Time: September 2008 to February 2009

IT WAS TIME OF FIGHTING LOVE

It was time of fighting love, the ultimate battle of of testerone and oestrogen magnified by the credit crunch, family feuds and birth of Kai.

The two people that I cared for themost were not there for me when I needed themmost, so why do I need them 'Angelina

'Its me, the cat and Kai from now on, we do not need you.' Angelina.

'If Don dies you will be the one to blame" Maria

"If she come and lives at the shop we will move back to London" Maria

'I have been running the shop for you and you are hardly ever here, instead you are running after her" Don

"You cannot run this business, it is best we sell it" Don

"After sacrificing 15 years of my life and creating income streams for you both in mind is this how you repay me?" Brad

'I have increased the turnover of this shop" Don

Lesson 3:

"Words can destroy your life and can have double edged meaning. Also some times words uttered have no value"

IT WAS THE TIME OF THE KAIBERNATOR

Time: March 2008 to May 2009

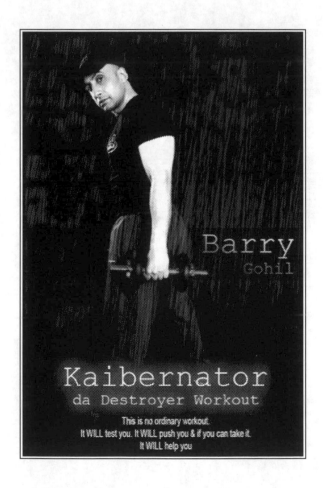

Barry
Gohil

Kaibernator
da Destroyer Workout

This is no ordinary workout.
It WILL test you. It WILL push you & if you can take it.
It WILL help you

IT WAS THE TIME OF THE KAIBERNATOR

Wise ones say that a baby can make or destroy a relationship.

It made Brad and Angelina realize how different they were, differences became magnified.

Brad and Angelina were never compatible however the property portfolio that they built from nothing held them together

There was always a lack of compromise uncertainty, and doubt.

In business Angelina always felt under minded by Brad. Also, Brad historically could never settle properly with Angelina.

So Kai was a relationship consolidation baby.

It's amazing how Kai makes your realize people perceptions.

Brad become redundant as a man.

Kai was taken away his dotting mum away from his dad to being her new life with David on the farm.

Brad was faced with a breakdown in relationships, debt and loss of income, he found work in the midlands however the income was not sufficient to cover his borrowings.

Brad had to make heart wrenching decisions. He made his way back to London and reclaim the house that was rented out.

Tenants had destroyed the house and caused 40 to 60k worth of damage. Brad found himself suicidal.

Brad found himself looking scruffy, with a large bread and he found himself sleeping in the same clothes days on end. He was in a mental state of collapse.

Lesson 4:

"A baby canmake or break / consolidate a relationship"

IT WAS A TIME TO OVERCOME THE FIGHT WITHIN

Time: June 2009 to September 2009

IT WAS A TIME TO OVERCOME THE FIGHT WITHIN

Brad contemplated suicide by drinking or by of taking drugs. The stress of several things collapsing in his world got the better of him.

Brad was invited to Kai's birthday up north on the farm.

Seeing David holding and sleeping with his son Kai on Kai's birthday got the better of him.

However, he controleed his emotions.

Angelina chose to be with David and there was a price to be paid.

Brad then met a friend in London who introduced him to a martial artist.

The martial artist spoke to Brad and told him the he experienced similar events where he lost his home, relationship.

The martial artist said get your backside to the gym.

So Brad hit the gym again.

It was a time to overcome the fight within, to face the man in the mirror amidst the credit crunch, family, relationship and financial issues.

It was time to unravel re-evaluate destructive thought process, emotions, habits; it was a time to make a further change, to transform.

To regain focus, clarification and direction.

It was a time to stop, drinking and eating junk food; It was a time to come back even harder and stronger to defy the odds . . .

Lesson 5:

"Life events can derail you where you can easily stray and take the wrong path'

IT WAS TIME TO RE:
TRAIN IN STEALTH MODE

Time: October 2009 to January 2010

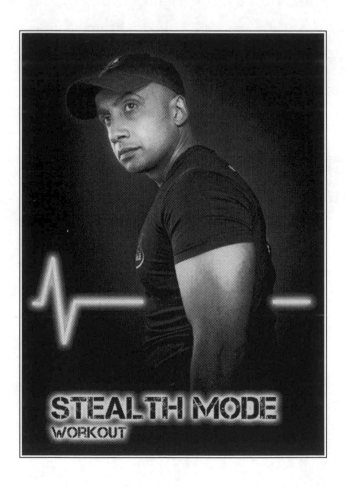

IT WAS TIME TO RE: TRAIN IN STEALTH MODE

Whilst in emotional, mental turmoil is was it was time to re-enter the gym and train quietly and confidently in stealth mode.

It was a time to re: seize the dumbbells and to re:create.

Brad trained hard channelling all the frustrations and anger of all the things that had collapsed in his life into his workouts.

He trained in stealth mode. He was all to aware of the evil eye and the decepticons: people who did not seem what they were around him.

Brad met people from all sorts of backgrounds who had been affected by the credit crunch.

Property professionals who were experiencing chest problems or who had heart attacks.

A friend of his contacted him out of the blue, his friend Peter lost 2 businesses and they wound up owing the banks money.

His wife fell into depression and wound up living abroad.

Brad met another friend where the power of emotions got the better of him and he hit his wife and wound up in prison and with a criminal record.

He also met men and women who had experienced the passport workout where they were used by their partners to secure their stay in the UK and saw the impact of this on their lives and saw the loss.

He met athletes who were helping a guy sell a propery portfolio worth 65 million.

Brad also read about high profile media case like that of Grant Bovey and Anthea Turner filing for Bankruptcy and experiences of chefs; Gorden Ramsey and Jamie Oliber, Nicholas Cage etc.

People of all social classes were impacted by the credit crunch in several ways.

Lesson 6:

"SELECT YOUR WEAPON OF MASS CREATION"

EYE OF THE TIGER

TIME: OCTOBER 2009 TO JAN 2010

EYE OF THE TIGER

It was a time to work out like the eye of the tiger.

Brad started to work out at high intensity.

Brad would workout until he sweated and reached the zone . . .

To enter the gym and identify dumbbells and machines and to attack them with great ferocity like the eye of the tiger with precision and with focus.

Lesson 7:

"TRAIN WIH PASSION, CHANNEL ALL THAT IS GOING WRONG IN YOUR LIFE AND CREATE POSITIVE ENERGY"

IT WAS TIME TO BUST A GUT

TIME: OCTOBER 2009 TO JAN 2010

IT WAS TIME TO BUST A GUT

Since September 2008 Brad had put on weight, it was a time to redevelop the core, to rebuild the core—the abs—to strengthen it by a series of workout s and by consuming power foods.

Food of the gods that energize.

Brad started to re ; purify his diet.

He had already transformed his mind set, and the body was getting there.

Lesson 8:

"RE BUILD A STRONG BASE, BUILD A STRONG CORE"

BEWARE OF THE VIXEN

TIME: OCTOBER 2009 TO JAN 2010

BEWARE OF THE VIXEN

Brad got approached several times by girls of all ages, however given Brads experience with Angelina it was a time to be aware of the vixen, her purpose to take the eye off the tiger, to take him off his momentum.

To entangle him into her world.

Lesson 9:

"THE VIXEN CAN TAKE YOU OFF MOMENTUM"

IMPROVE THE GRIP

TIME: OCTOBER 2009 TO JUNE 2010

IMPROVE THE GRIP

Brad started to further improve, strengthen the grip, by a series of exercises and further mould the mind set and body.

Brad then met a friend from his work days. A wise man called Cole.

He told Brad that we are living in world that is designed to stress.

His friend Cole said that life is about choice . . . you have to options either take a pill of creation—where you constantly create and take a pill of destruction where you will die and lead a path of self destruction.

Brad's friend Cole started to teach him the lesson of serenity.

Lesson 10:

"THROUGH EXERCISE YOU SLOWLY IMPROVE YOUR GRIP ON YOUR MIND AND BODY AND LIFE EVENTS"

CONNECT TO THE HIGHER POWER

TIME: JUNE TO NOVEMBER 2010

CONNECT TO THE HIGHER POWER

Brad started to enter the spiritual world, through his workouts and contant sweating, by challenging his mind and body, he formed the mind and body connection. With the guidance of Cole he was learning serenity.

Through the intensity of the workouts a surge spiritual energy, chi, kundalini, passed through his body, a new spiritual voice was speaking to Brad.

To detach from all emotional bonds and material woes.

It was a time to listen to the inner voice, to see the light to feel connected to the mighty one.

It was a time where the mind and body connected to the heavens.

It was a place of peace and abundance where all problems were no more.

It was time to listen to, trust the inner voice.

Brad's workouts were no longer physical he discovered chi or spiritual energy.

He had visions of heaven and souls and that we humans were all being guided by Gods.

The God were channelling good and bad energies into us.

However, the God were channelling their energies it was done to us—man or woman to choose the right or wrong path.

Lesson 11:

"FORM A MIND BODY CONNECTION WITH THE HIGHER BEING. DEVELOP CHI OR KUNDALINI."

WATCH ONES BACK

TIME: NOVEMBER 2010 TO DECEMBER 2010

WATCH ONES BACK

It was time to watch ones back

It was time to watch ones back.

By now Brad had identified and formed alliances with angels . . . or agents of change and to form the inner circle.

It was a time where Brad had mastered his mind, body and emotions and reached a point of self realisation.

Lesson 12:

"FORM A CIRCLE OF FRIENDS WHO YOU CAN TRUST, WORK AND GROW WITH"

IT WAS TIME TO BECOME A MAN

BE A MAN

Lesson 14:

"EACH ONE OF YOU IS A HERO THAT IS WAITING TO BE BORN OR REBORN"

BE A SUPERHERO IN YOUR LIFE

BE A SUPERHERO IN YOUR LIFE

Brad had come a long way since 2008 when his world collapsed around him.

It was time for the birth of a new superhero the emergence of Breakfast Barry.

His goal to motivate, inspire people to face life's challenges and to transform, turn their lives around to defy the odds to regain and maintain focus of their mind, diet and exercise and life goals.

When worlds, economise, relationships collapse it is a time to self reflect too see the man in the mirror, to work out in stealth mode, to take a grip, to resist the temptations of the vixen, to listen to the inner spiritual voice to create a new you.

Lesson 14:

FACE LIFE'S CHALLENGES

When the world is against you—the Banks, relationships, your family, partner, when chips are stacked against you.

It is time to realise that less is more and that your health is your wealth, your mental, spiritual and physical health.

It is a time to take stock and lift, overcome the burden, defy the odds.

Brad met a social worker who said that normally it takes 3 things to go wrong in your life before you have a breakdown.

Brad told the social worker but what if six or more life events get the better of you then what?

The social worker said: well I would expect that person NOT to be standing or living.

Brad said to the social worker: well that person was me.

The social worker looked at Brad in disbelief and amazement.

Summary

Brad's Learning:

- If you are an entrepeauner or considering a move or having a baby do not rely on the banks have an emergency fund.

- Banks are run by people who make costly mistakes.

- Beware of close ones around you—family and friends.

- Dreams can collapse.

- Life does not always go as planned.

- Do all the things that you are passionate about and enjoy.

- Family and friends can emotionally blackmail you.

- Be around people that will help, support and nurture you.

- Create a supportive team.

- If you are not compatible in a relationship get out fast.

- Beware of the evil eye.

- There are no guarantees in relationships so have a contract an agreement and make provisions if you have a child.

- Where materialistic things are concerned get things written up.

- Keep an eye on your pennies. A penny makes a pound.

- Where one thing or several things are being destroyed create.

- Looking after you physical and mental health for that is all you have.

- Constantly find solutions to problems and come out of your comfort zOne.

- Pray to God the creator for he will show you a way.

- Do not let the power of emotions get the better of you.

- Learn about the power of exercise.

- The world is experiencing a Shiva affected where there is constant, rapid destruction and creation.

- Moments can shape your life.

- Each one of you of is a superhero waiting to transform.

COMING SOON

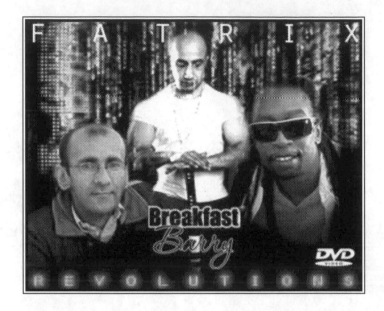

Award winning film where one man defies.

A film based on true events.

ABOUT THE AUTHOR

B. Gohil is BSc (Hons) qualified and has already written the Breakfast Barry Story, 2010.

He has been featured in health and fitness publications, TV, and radio and has been to events like Body Power, Vitality, B Fit Expo. He is author, speaker, and trainer and also does a lot for charities.

Since the economic crisis of 2008, he has met thousands of people from all walks of life that have inspired him to write this book.

He has discovered through knowing that his father had a heart attack that through the power of the mind, exercise, and diet, the body has the capacity to heal itself and recover. The body is also a temple of the spirit. It is the spirit that allows you to create.

B. Gohil has lived in Africa, UK, USA, and extensively traveled to Europe and the Far East.

B. Gohil lives in Ilford, Essex, London, UK.